KILDARE

KILDARE

✦

Stacy Doris

ROOF BOOKS
NEW YORK

ISBN: 0-937804-59-2
Library of Congress Catalog Card No.:

Design by Deborah Thomas.
Cover from the video *Teatime* by Melissa Smedley.

Versions of some of this work have appeared in *hole, Phoebe, Big Allis, Conjunctions, Chain, Raddle Moon*, and *Torque*; grateful acknowledgment to the editors and publishers.

Thanks to Chet Wiener, and Robert Kocik for close readings, and to Toni Simon, Brighde Mullins, Melanie Neilson, Nick Piombino, and Ann Lauterbach for their prodigious supportiveness.

Thanks also to the Fund For Poetry for an award which added necessary writing time.

Dedicated, with love, to Myrna Ruskin Doris and Sidney Doris

This book was made possible, in part, by a grant from the New York State Council on the Arts and the National Endowment for the Arts.

Roof Books
are published by
Segue Foundation
303 East 8th Street
New York, New York 10009

ARCTIC UNCLES (ON ROLLERBLADES) ADVANCE

KILDARE

ARCTIC UNCLES (ON ROLLERBLADES) ADVANCE

FEATURES THESE UNGLUED
(AND FUNKY) CHARACTERS:.

Military Yann

Many-named Uncle(s)

Teen boy rollerblade groups (The only sane ones of the bunch)

Lassie Twin Nieces

TiK, a military cuteness *gamink*

Reinforcements

Transportation, arctic circles,

loony island w/

Intestine-bon-bon Factory.

Bon Courage!

FIRST CHANCE

Probe Droids SUCK!

Unc. helped Yann with the igloo setup,

popsicle version.

Soothing: "Don't worry: the sounds are way distant."

As ice thins —

the background shakes —

obfuscating *Leap of Wrath*.

Live die and what not.
Lie down and crawl off.

Available (echo) AVAILABLY:

Tundra Blitz:

OH SWEET,

AGENT madness, bit of Latin revenge (yes-'um asked for)

New World Comp #.

Mighty Virgin Alert.

MUNCHED ON THE LAGOON...

(blued) elkboys autosuck

flammable?

Why the hat?

TiK glides, from snowcap, down to their mobile

(with a (cold) pizza)

Chanted:

GORE	OX	Chris	Scissor
8	8	6	8

In playability and shift.

Enthused, Uncle orders

un psycho-style salon

for to reverse the brains of two *lassies*

sipping insults

'til they're sugar-crazed, hot

and see what's on their minds:

neck-tethered, caressed to pieces.

The ULTIMATE *Gamin/Gamine* rag

TOYFIGURE Comeback — Free!

Pull me out uncle H.

Bad Uncle, bad
stocking stuffer

growls: *bring the kids round.*

Meanwhile: An occurrence like urine

A — ummm . . . urinous occurrence

medically proves

centerfold with secret fats

COMMANDO

super putty/ super tip . . .

Lophead. You.

Win: Mr. Bad get rearranged!

Excuse me Miss . . .

Uncle! (TiK) Multiply:

the lotus carpet's hideous.

Down its hatch, goes:

Authority creams/
thighbangling duel over newdom's crown emerald.

With the Demos ride naughty,

certain lasso bad.

Curious Uncle Roy, banned in Utah

(ammo films)

what a close shave!

Star Products test/ results in uncle Stinky

Stinky ... here!

Home-picking and original
begs, upholds many

(they specialize in privates)

European-type: notches   All itsy
deductible, register

NOW, *girrrrls!*

(panorama shy)

the Asian blue extrusion

Off Limits, *Gums Apart*

first class scramble.

Hey Marvin: the brain drug's proved elusive!

Gotcha backs.

Laments: *MY icon bean — Neurospunk —*

(Half-man but all caution):

hamburgering over it

(a nanosplit dawning)

TAKES RIDES

(sonic female champ)

IV VR TM

. . . Mmmmmm, ask the Virtutects.

Overhead arrival: Hey!

Adrenaline-hot mam's'

twit vision

priestly, glazed as all that.

Gamine Heaven

Thanks much.

Bunny one in each size goes.

Uncle: Try spending it all in one place!

Sample charts:

CLASSIFIED: Petting under/ same old rodent

      Imp above/ option tail

      Bulky with/ tonic

      Stand back!

      (Oooo NANA!)

Big dominions have just what
comes out of a plug up.

MYSTERY . . . PEEL here.

In Uncle's preview wigwam reigns ENvironmental wattage.

OVermouth's
Heather mcfur in auto venture

(Pandemonium IN-CORp)

Saga logs on all 64 bits pounding, recites

A SORRY TALE:

of mega-bulbed nymphs await

pre-wounded so feckless

bruised-in-tattoo, a trifle,

100% offer. Luck of the draw:

. . . A glimpse of darling entrails, prune sacrifice chides

and when they look for her — poof!

                              (echo)   poof

Forget Stephan. Forget
all the not-there guys forgot.

YO: dumbbells that explode!

Parachute whole!

(The *National* ocean).

SO, Urethraejacked boy-bomb:

Any further questions?

In double-come electrodes, Unc.

was choo-choo-spliced out. Yep.

Later Able-mapped suburb, with colorless bilge ancient . . .

QUICK the jar:

messages: Wait for *Me* specter

while Matrix is Navigate

(the ethanol champs)

A Flash: Smutwalls and pincushions TEAM UP
in a wake, of remedy-scattershot:

Pyramid wolf hide-away.

Mind-sweeper

Awesome posse:

Ask a harem:

                      (echo).

(Lands)

"In next to nothing"

rolled use - whatever —

pointing, 17, tidy-but-hard,

Experienced Richness.

. . . . .

Dizzy 17 prong, solo-attached,

whose needed/ an account of TiK:

Odd, browner, naturally,

glum. Jubilant: where

a bellboy in sight, or belief

at a nature precinct eat quickly!

(Lands)

A serious talk, but with no leg to stand on

bender dummies up/ crush dummies

come along and go to pieces.

In a rush careen bounty scam

upsets the creature model.

A HOMUNCULUS VIEWPOINT

(realistic fluid) moves

(in this case, small)

inch by inch!

Face out.

Yes! Enter UNCLE today!

KEY   wigs/ quest/ flab/ crank dream = power.

Wimpy bit (12)

Something to gobble on.

Screeched feline control wets
the whole blowing system:

Advance invincibility

and secret   echo fodder and

grow Napalm!

The LaComa Knight in Bizyland configurates.

Infinite *Lives*.

Money - up. No timer.

Heave-Ho and a thimble of fog

(in a past option) penultimate kindling.

And, exclusive, 10-gal chances.

The dragon-flare romp.

Hey: Wannabes: Can they Lie, Steal, Bash,

Navigate half-legged

shoot from a cannon for a living, or what?

High-Jinx Island.

Elephant: #1

(Lambs)

Slices and creams Betty alongside Jill
soaking their venom (own) marinara UP.

Good girls are fried girls, icing on — Right, uncle?

In a row,

a rippling muscle valley

both side to back.

Turbine fat mush (says)   to a little pinch

in the climax undercut

lacy without being:

Prison jerk   backslat

tremor color   freed arm

bang (in close)   supple rotor

lips illumined   claw kiss

disappointment   saber lap

Choose cuddle now.

     down

     both down

     left down.

SECOND GAME

Loaded with new enemies,

cool dialogue, jeeps,

a slew of pocket-sized Yanns

shall battle the permafrost.

The aim: archeology

boom-remote thunder.

Warning:

All Previous Survivors have Lost it.

Reminder: To all — Lassie Twins:

Good Nieces are petted;

you can be your own assailant

just up the volume to swap lives

with a real princess.

IONA, now they call her,

thirsty from electron wads

Frank Uncle currency,

goes bareback, spurred horseless

poultry whip; the Booby Prize:

Now Possibly = Corrodes.

**YANN: Catch the
TWINS! They're dangling:**

Sick picture; delay.

The barbecue link

distant members uniformed

intervals, regular, pausing

to separate the holes (2 by 2).

Big machine

sisters, legitimately oiled

switch minigates.

Continent, in a net, size-wired, lusty:

with vitamin gloss/

getting in the act:

seen: Stiff, religious, foul

multiplied tips.

Out splaying, empty:

What next, Detective?

Ditto heads *Slag*

Thrashing for buttons

and iotas, they chomp. This ain't Yann's first

denomination screw-in.

60 Fields per Second.

Recordbending heat is unportable now,

also known as shockless; mini.

Slender

guarantees

an adviral digit

the cell's oscillation:

TIRED   **BETTER**

interaction   crime

adhesive   surrogate

free   ambient

thought   window

medicate   rainforest

love   audition

In *imagi*NATION

TiK and Yann hook up, hit it off, /and

within moments:

She's nicked him

he's strapped her

she boffs him

he leaks/ he drenches her

with Crisco

she crackles

he flips.

OTHER: flatten/ hang/ spread/ zing/ glove/ sizzle.

Bushwhack Sign Up Here

LETS UNCLE Input, capture, display

mix and produce

that's what friends are for.

A worry-free professional, finger tips — easy in

overnight receipt.

TiK, attacker turned iffy

invites/ one hope to outwit

El Commandeer ('Dong').

Helpful explosive surprises clue TiK

(gritty back view)

CLOSER.

On loose in the COCONET

One little guy shaves off time

for the brawny.

They IN AURORA/ LAND
(Where Sighted = Destroy)

Uncle happens

upon a Weirdo Mechanic AREA

for pantyline reconnaissance

(with chats progress easy):

. . . Flexing lifelike but cuter, Miss LIBERTY toasts

now to lucid cycle slits abound

pedal feel-ya camping

for come and gnaw on   /public

genitorture fest times 3

vivid whiffs
organic hardware, juiced

tames, bound is only the start.

Along with Yann, snap up Uncle:

young, oral.

UNCLE, Welcome to Stealthland

    (a.k.a. Shangri-La)

bigger than *Swiss* and totally Verboten.

When Hushcraft touch down

on Groom Path

the limits drizzle

(legend, plus mini footage)

magpie romance complete.

A Silent invitation/ Jockey withers style

Catacombs use vices
(By the dozen).

Nice bridal set up/ coyly unlatched

okaying death nozzles in irresolute pits.

Dustbowl Wakendudes (sentries)

for the mothercam vigil

A Story Illusion.

C'mon Down!

The ridges are prickly;

unwelcome civilians get exchanged

in those bushes.

Moonlight huskless Reminder:

the fittest are gun-shy;

go elsewhere.

But UFO hobbyists/ would vacation in

a classified facility, too bad.

And tough luck Uncle

basketball sized yolks evidenced.

. . .Three lost Vikings, them lost souls:

walk right off cliffs into traps,

downright nasty!

A fake gamble ensues,

sweet reason circuit

Warlords toolbox

including horror and blood leash.

Wigman, an undead

(gothic role-playing theme)

made off from the party with the amulet and radishes

and automap case;   hit the road

to Missing Thought Plantation.

Meanwhile Connectivity flaunts, isthmus-wide.

Triads and other spiritual pollutants flock

overcoming growth

to indecisive shine. Meanwhile nibble:

TiK's pearl delta skin system

or Trancelab convert

ready to love

the MUD cataclysm.

AN ASSORTMENT OF MYSTICS

radio-hostile

full of grumpiness hovers, pins, reels back home

roosting in custody, by night,

poised on an arrow/ but with a tendency to slip.

But its Lonely at the Top

After gorilla inhalation

what's left of Monkey Island?

The High Dollars breakthrough primrose,

carbon freezing boredom.

Either connect the dots

or push Uncle off. He boomerangs.

As Uncle Tubby angers

in a handicapped second

do the guck pelvis.

At Shiver Headquarters:

The action by ice breath

collaborates

against tiny youthful i.d. duo.

Advance to R&R Depot

(Star Ranch joint vacation)

More fun than nipping off TiK's fingers.

P. S.: AT THE FAIR:

Human Beehive admission loots

Tragedy Cylinder Attraction:

World's Largest Crackerjack (w/ rest settee on top).

Prize Unfinished.

Wanted: a can opener.

Automatic-Tiny

(The double-nothing sisters)

Mulch dropsy combat

get dangerous from ease.

Unleash Terrier

(And now, the infection)

Uncle won't rest before he rules

compound Insidious:

Toss your partner into a fence

do-se-do your partner

and wallop

with the brutal stroke

twice before landing.

A hug/smash combo

Midair teleport

fakes out of nothing

icky reptile device.

TiK-as-Valkyrie

pie-throw endeavors

jumps, lands senseless

(indigestion attached).

The flowers squirting contest.

X-tra Innings: The Twins' Last Metamorphosis

Three doggie tornadoes

crop up record firing

along — too bad for them — soporific hillsides.

Leap from the skateboard

jiggle positions

(they're heavy).

Elsewhere Poodle Gorgeous

bobs in unknown platforms

helplessly jell-o.

LAST CHANCE [Includes (souvenir) Documents]

SOMEHOW Uncle unearthed

The *Blush Swill's Codex*:

a (whining)

unpraised fissure

chalky, flightless, but live

(w/ pupa display

of wearying awareness

in strips of bewilderment)

then top it off with fangs! Several and exact,

a petrification treatise

on throb, salivate, cascade.

Falling Stones deaden stairways;

the feather impressions

grind to a halt in sea plastic.

An ilex crust, limpid

forages by snail patch, in quantities

and omission.

Scum Dating (The *Swill Codex* Made Simple)

Err Period: glaucous and carbonate

lower, oval-dotted, glides

its calamitous battalion,

puerile cut. Rounded off.

Surely magnanimous.

Surely aquatint.

And, immutably, steaming-but-equal.

. . . . .

(p. 2):

Waddling remains were after volcanic.

In coiled jaws/ bright fern.

AT THE PEBBLE-APPARENT WRECK (in Future)

Through lung eyes, glistening still

diorama mossing depths

faintly opens equal, turned to a clam age.

TiK-famous. Spiffed

yummy marathon sleuth

for animal outskirts hunt.

A SEAWEED ARMATURE/ BACKDROP ILLUSION:

Earth, out of sight,

cutsey roused

(in "swamp treasure").

PETRIFIED DESERT SPLINTER (Biotoxic Mission)

TiK on detailed target

copiously, kill

in a universer crank

good pop rate, but spoiled by weather.

THE INTRUDER COMPANION

scattered pods

lop and cut

lop and cut

they sure do.

DATA LIBRARY (Fungal Agenda)

(*Because Yann's capabilities shape every TiK's sortie.*)

Need to know.

If Yann's meat finder's up/ TiK don't leave flank exposed.

If multi-aspect/ TiK, don't leave, period.

Sub or over-sonic misses/ stump the aura.

Yann hang low/ then TiK clutter

timing Gage/ agog.

If he's close to bingo/

TiK press;

pump compare.

ORDER: (TiK's) Dream(land)

In a high-rez battle suit

plunge, roll, bank, soar, lose never.

G-force activate

one proto-star flexi-kid transforms

gentle dose

for infodeck patriarch's insanity. ('Dong'.)

Bobs and weaves.

Beddie pie.

(*Prays*)

bled amateur,

dig in now.

Assignment: Grab the controls/ spread Democracy

it's time.

Accurate and loaded, the Toucan Craw brig

is tactile/ a maverick

ashram-equipped.

It pays to sweat bullets:

Fly higher/ fly longer — obsolescent pilot.

TiK's radarless sidewind pairs.

Surprise Map

(For cheat-enabled basis.)

A double-flawless whack

should do the job.

If not: reptile endurance.

If not: womanly harpoon.

Therefore, TiK glows, later on

(in the chair)

resinous.

A hit.

The General ('Dong"s) Notebook

(Peek-a-boo sadistic)

A hook 'em up factory

gnaws victims with suspense.

Detailed operating costs

(derision of the navels)

blood's merely an hors d'oeuvre

torture morsel.

All hooked submissivies to parachute direct

to this boudoir of malevolence, ready.

A slush fund of veterans

ether-ripened for the privilege . . .

Dig in, boys.

TiK's Entry 3 (Illustrated)

Oh, loony-dump islet

the intestine bon-bon factory

cuts excess with poison

and in deformation thrills.

A gore ideologue

'Dong' works out a system

for interchangeable pickling

'til the corpses beyond recognition

can serve equally.

Final Stages ('Dong''s Tally Sheet)

The victim gets messy

s/he's cannibalized by invisible romanceers

and, in slug rewire

paralyzed except for the tongue

idiot blithers

salivary mud

to carry taint

in very lowest microbes

the necorphilous aftermath.

May 8th, TiK Continuing

Reached swamp peninsula.

Everywhere silt,

the fungus night breeds

low faces sucked to absence

bathed in vermin-retch pools

degeneracy saline

nitrous can-can floor-show.

Act 2.

Guzzled the tea.

Now sealed from inside

its bullets palpitate

unparticle crease.

Remove from oven.

Come Kiss Uncle 'Dong'

Body mold hatching

out he pops

slimmed a tad,

webbed handshake grapples

good as new.

Instructions:

Vibrate tourists well.

They splice them in clusters.

Uncle 'Dong' tapes himself

back into comfy egg.

Then speechless and determined

to rig havoc, rolls.

Shove 'Em or Shave 'Em (The Loony Island Crew)

Lush, but afflicted

by a rescue-hungry germ

Uncle Redundant trades

his parts among himself

the remnants for cheap

delivery hazards

fated ruby deal.

Over by the slot machines

Uncle Ghoul loafs

beaming his "core"

into the pinballs of others. Recruits.

A flair for weaknesses

the joy-pain gadget

reinauguration.

What Base

Reckon lucked alarm

island-wide jerking

gave up their coordinates

fuel: mined and ashen

pouts, tinkles catastrophic.

Hey who did that:

let TiK get real toasty.

TiK Kracks

("Pardon the Scram")

Pulverized comrades

bathed by insect phosphor scums

in a puff of marrow cloud

in a skull-mash dollop

but quietly, tranquil,

and with body parts removed:

spout new virals

never to colonize.

After, Select Hero

(a touch-tone alternative)

Who drives the boys senseless with his or her

hammer plus nails.

Placid, though saucy

which the group bubbles panic from.

KILDARE

A *MYSTICAL* DEDICATON. OR, Life of VACANT KID. And his WHOLE Race.

Now more transparent, in a hothouse

on dishes grows:

abandoned the rebound, coughed up and held captive

for its seed

Not to eat! (*Ripens in drying; explodes.*)

(*Sung.*) "the interior light"

(*Whispering.*) — Take advantage now, harder!

(*Sung.*) . . . "not outside; blessed with phosphorescence . . ."

Crushed the peach, in a strange osmosis.

(*Sucks. Sucks longer.*)

(*Misses the pit. Continues. Gives thanks:*)

Thanks, and condolences.

(*Sound of slap. Pause.*) — Again! (*Sound of slap, limping.*)

(*Improves.*)

Just a little love, twice a day. (*Sneaks up behind.*)

the whole bag of tricks —

Childless still. Pounded

on the rim.

* * *

Daydream much, Lockhead?
Nope.
Then you're a lucky man. And a bachelor?
To boot.

Synopsis of KILDARE

(Motley sketch of everything that has never been believed):

Sheila is a talk show hostess whose luster can't make up for her crummy sense of timing. Nonetheless worshipped, full of karma, ambitions, and cash, she sallies forth in quest of past lives during the course of minor surgery (a mere routine procedure), while under the influence of a local (anesthetic).

From an Arcadian operating scenario Sheila's consciousness spins back through a series of past lives (mostly her own) in the guise (not in chronological order) of a petty thief, Benedictine (captured by pirates), "All Gums" Evelyn, Tinkerbell (down home), Homecoming Queen, a contortionist, Herself - but zapped to Mars, and other girl champion archetypes.

After a brief interview, soul search, reminiscences, and Time Trip (a stroll down involuntary memory lane), Sheila stumbles at length upon the real New Age (future and post-nuclear) where, incarnated as Carmen, she takes a central part (that of Good) in a struggle against the crazy Doctor Kildare, right in the midst of his gamble for universal (what remains of it) leadership. Due to shape-shifting, an equivocating slave, and other set-backs, the duel ends in a draw (though Sheila maintains an upper hand). Kildare is dissolved (or is he?).

Finally, in any case, in a triumphal cross of bliss with unemployment, in the spirit(s) of beating and joining both, Sheila merges with the (putrid, stinking) half-life of the still moldering Kildare, giving rise (before it's too late) to a prodigious chorus of somewhat interchangeable (36 - 24 - 36) nurses who, along with their ever-faithful servant-breeder Klink, make off to the pastoral eternity of laughing gas.

(*Trumpets.*)

Character Equivalents (Dramatis Personae)

Sheila:	Kildare:	Slave:
a.k.a. (a petty thief)	Franky/ Johnny	Vacant Kid
Benedictine (pirates' captive)	Warden	KLINK
"All Gums" Evelyn	His "Majesty"	Woodsman
Tinkerbell	Ecoman	
Homecoming Queen	Lady Murasaki	
Contortionist	Doc	
Herself, dumped on Mars		
CARMEN		
Nurse Chorus		
Nurse Sorceresses (1 & 2)		

Assorted Other Characters (Mostly Sheila's relatives or rescuers or Sheila herself, in some harder-to-pin-down incarnation.)

Soba

Troll ("Savant")

Blue Cousins

Edrin

Mutants

The Invisible

THE CAMEO APPEARANCE BY A TALK SHOW HOSTESS (AND HER PAST LIVES)

SHEILA Interviewed

SHEILA: Johnny and me, we go . . .

A Mouth. - Mud -

Resulting when teddy bear claws

inflammation

Frank sighs —

. . . to dream of entry in two spots at once, in a many-tried
method grasp

sucking (or licks) as Attractive
and simple

Franky   —   Frank

Franky   —   Frank

Franky

with slapping

and both sides wet, now testing one-

toothed.

Sheila's Feelings Beyond

First, a tickling thru needles

(over 40, monstrous)

ramped around the throat and then down, down

where fingers punch through for breath
in eddying recesses

HIS: inhumanly quick from desperation
HERS: inhumanly quick every time

And, suddenly, she couldn't breathe (old beams the afternoon;

a ceiling caves) Granted: bad water; granted: the fuse;

she locates the blockage, punches a hole through — HE: from the

side now/rejamming fingers — SHE: might collapse, instead rips

OR: sensation left her legs, she quick

     seized with teeth

     and, as he dies, gives in to her own pain

cleanses herself, leaves the girl in

better hands

Oh, but she'd observed J's tongue then (nothing stops that)

pickling inside

And asked how such a sight

ever arranged

Softening —

66

Sheila, *post-Shipwreck*

becoming a prow

(or sacrifice)

cut the ropes/ not their daughter.

How her grip weakens

How her grip weakens Dad's legs . . .

Cut the cord!

Beth, impulsively hid in the well
while the virus instructs
these mad couplings

(*bottomless with trolleys*)

(psst — the beastly disease that claims . . .)

and mom-as-illustration

on fours beside the diagram

obeys, next

bubbles

feet first in hunger.

EVEN SO

On both sides, in the spiritual way,

as said, the breasts were props.

TIME TRIP

Scene I:

SHEILA: (*in the violator's head*

      meaning reptilian, slinky.)

        You fail! (*aside*) before being given much chance.

        (*Raises whips.*)

   J.:   (*gets in line with the other hooded forms*).

        Waits for DOOMSDAY.

        (*Sobs, soft.*)

        Doesn't think twice. Done thinking.

SHEILA: And now that we're happy, totally, whadda we do now?

JOHNNY: Take a vacation?

(II: *Pretty desert*)
The trysting tree trysts. The trysting tree cleaves, and all the rest oozes. Sequence of toasts and splashings. A shadow falls.

(II a.: *'The Dawn'.*)

Land of Our Forebears, but do-able.

Several of Sheila's past lives *Enter* and *Exit*. She salutes.

Sheila as ancient cult figure; stuck. Johnny pulls her out, physically, as from quicksand.

Snapshots: Johnny-as-captain.

Johnny-as-cameraman.

Sheila in onepiece. Sheila in garters. Sheila in chains. The legs open. Morsels.

SHEILA: (*plaintive*). Scratch me! No, lower (*more plaintively*). Ah!

(*Trecks across time.*)

(*Memories from opera plots.*)

(*A flurry of postcards.*)

Meanwhile, in their dreams, and when they're meditating, the tragedies tune
in, i.e.,

a Marketplace for Sacrifices

(*Gags one sister while mincing up the other.*)

SEE EVE DROOL BLOOD!

Guess which the droopy servant offers next on her tray —

What were the leftovers before?

(*as backdrop*) SHEILA: Where's the welcome crew?

JOHNNY: Oh, shut up.

(*Quibbles and Old Abuse.*)

Later SHEILA (*reviving*) forages for miracles.

Return to Scene I.

the PORTRAITS as *GIRL CHAMPIONS*

HEISTS:

A Long Island mansion, lynx in the hand

found dead, the mind out, wouldn' let her quit

on metal shell training

to switch back home - in slacks

all that litter — humph.

Wait a sec.

Later . . .

    A.K.A.: *(Fully restrained.)*

    WARDEN: *(as nurse; false angelic).*

          All better?

    A.K.A.: *(dopey).* Good, it feels good,

          it feels carnival, General.

Next thing — footwork

a.k.a. — ouf!

Take, that.

. . . double-crossed with spite and dark, expensive secrets.

Poor, hostage, Benedictine

Captive-cum-empress in pirate fleet dome

('else it's back to the slave trade for females

and Latin kids)

She's forced to sip, gussied

up, pinned down.

Come give her a clue, a penny.

Head lube and oil change —then—

speaking only gibberish

martinis her way home.

(She could break you like a pencil,

sweet touch-me heart-o.)

Thud

here goes/

everyone's only chance.

. . . In the most SENSUAL LIMBO *Ride*:

Hey! Milkers!

(*they squirt the glass with mama-whip*)

SAP, that is, baby food,

IS TASTY!

. . .

EVELYN, all GUMS

(don't dare call her 'Miss')

REMOVES the TEETH,

INHALES every drop.

Hot, boiling —

Why watch when you can lick?

DOWN HOME: Real Anterior Riches

OR **Beautiful tropical plant in full bloom seeks**

Nurseryman (seeder) to watch for measurement:

THE NYMPH-ISLE Antidote

No, menace these days

Bored on the ROCKS seeks

a nipple's reasonings, a staple

underground sum

the length of all chocolate

times each of its instances, sigh-enlarged

(and later, by extra)

in turgid permanence

Why's Captain afraid

to see Nell's joints quadrupling? she says

it feels okay —

They mask and net in mermaid there
though out too long and tropic scars
the teeth fresh, soft perking.

Next, guava-round, our Homecoming Queen

(w/ her density oscillate)

marched to this system

(figured her nylons kept liturgically down)

in an Emancipation outfit

(landscape stuffed in the bust props)

and with numerous floats, old time

(extra blossoms, the innovation: a sliding)

pace that upsets all;

its pounds scramble at the rear to uphold —

this favorite string
pulls light then.

Circus Girl, then, drowning

in mid-performance (a violation)

shinnied to the dead point awoke

self-peeled

obligatory roulette, one-a-day

(circus girl's toy-zone) notched

by its tumble.

THE LEASH —- Grommet C:

The Leash — pirouette, somersault,

orders indifference, mattering regular

skins herself but won't strip

woebegone, a bride/

glued tight.

COME TO TAKE HER BACK

So, better join them.

The eye w/o pupil

and darn, on Mars dropped

(in less weight: bad stomach)

WHY Blue Man's vision
should BOTHER Sheila?

(in her transparent yellows) — All marionettes —

And if she don't feel like it?

Stoic fellow,

gets this situation's gravity

(though parasites its outcome)

desperate lunge in a fog
or a ketchup

and from sundry reports in need of an extra —

SHEILA: Why wouldn't any old girl do?

Post-post nuclear COMBAT across NEVER-NEVER LAND

MONEY vs. Organs (or, KILDARE REVISITED)

Begins on gasps: rapid, allergic:

*(Doc "Majesty" asleep, in a pile
dresses rubber.)*

With the way his metabolism spins

and the nipples remove to show

drowning nasturtiums, or less . . .

*(The nurse abandoned under a shelf, gagged
while her masked sisters combat
the genetic experiments.)*

Enter, THE INVISIBLE: Now, for Kildare!

      Take him to the cryogenic cell.

(. . . and two levels higher:)

      Evacuate!

KILDARE: I think I see why everyone looks alike now!

      I can still feel the pain of my (her) lung

      being yanked from my (her) chest.

      I know why the dwarf's nick-named "Tremble".

No side effects. None.

(*Kildare winks.*)

(*Inset*: The DOC (who melted down some in ex-nuclear rain): (*poised and grins*). Here goes! My chance to whip Sexy to pieces.

(*Grumbles heard from the opponents.*)

CARMEN: (*breaking in*). Quick! A power cell

       or Kildare (and the whole she-bang) will die!

(She doesn't realize: his cracked proclivities.)

Later, and miles off, in architectural safety
at Kildare's lab (or den) in the pit:

KILDARE: I'm on to save the race.

(*Aside: laughter.*)

CARMEN: But the cell wasn't found.

KILDARE: Then combat!

CARMEN: What about the Blob's indomitable slave-squad?

KILDARE: Get them.

* * *

Misguided Carmen and her sisters (plus their Blue-Man cousins)

a whole gang of Pusses in Boots, but more practical:

they're scared. In the distances

rebel patrols huddle. And mutants, traps, poison streams, mutants

heat, pinchings, mutants and MORE.

LOST IN THE ONE-TIME FOREST . . .

Damnation! (or Downtown) followed by a flood

and the Troll-device Net

a triple-crossing

in which Carmen

falls for this contemporary hunk-mutant guy

(Kildare would (and maybe will) stamp out his likes)

while the others — Soba, Edrin, Blue, Cousins all —

luck out, finding a sewage pipe, tumble down

(*gingerly*), hope Carmen's all right.

. . . She even calls his mutant dad (a lumpy dwarf) 'Kute'.

What's big boy's name? —Klink.

Height? —Six-six and upwards.

Acid-dimpled, blistered, with a cowlick perm.

The troll hums some waltzes. (Nick-name *Savant*.)

Carmen: SING ALONG!

She's ready (kids, truck, a ranch) for *n'importe*;

built to settle down

but maybe too slow?

Doc nabs them on the monitor; can't believe

his crystal — pawing — he fumes.

. . . Meanwhile, tuneful, humid, and adangle:

SOBA: Grip, Blue! Hold on! And don't look now - but —

(The stones, each a shark, or worse,

flash reptilian.)

CARMEN: But there's a world out

there, beyond these putrid conduits.

KLINK: Gosh, you're pretty.

Complex S.

Remove the lip plate and

smack — a freckled export kiss.

Remove the breast plates:

she's one among thousands,

collects defeats, back-slithering.

Gagged: sometimes.

So feisty and tenacious.

* * *

Initiating, Kildare multiplies.

SOBA: Hey!

KILDARE: Mission Accomplished.

She'll be kept as a specimen, though.

(*Throttles her.*)

SOBA: Yeah. Fine. Go ahead.

SAME Time, SOME Place.

SAVANT: Ullm . . . ulummmmmm (*prophetizes*)

    there's more on the way.

    But unless he gets human

    their fates turn.

Meanwhile, same CRITTER,

(*far off and underground*) wakens, stretches

and (thanks to poor planning)

the SLAVE returns, hobbles,

unzips most of his skin

so he's naked, but identical (Klink).

(*Calls to be remodeled*):

    Doc-maniac! Doc sloppy!

    Yes, and in record time.

    All better now, except

    for the indelible death marks of course.

SLAVE: (*Speaks from the ooze.*)

Fix me up Doc,

make me human for once!

I wanna be one of them.

KILDARE: I saw you die!

Slave (KLINK): Well I'm back now.

Though kept alive for decades

as experimental tissue

nipped, green accessless

clinically gone

(*whistles*) . . . what you done for me so far.

* * *

KILDARE: And what of the old mood swings?

SLAVE: Just pull the switch!

ELSEWHERE, in a Time Vise:

"Sequence completed."

The overblown molecules,

they pink and veer at Carmen's feet

as she eddies . . . down . . .

CARMEN: (*psychedelically*). PLEase

       don't zap me back to the creep reptiles again!

       And stop that twirling!

       (What a DRAG.)

(It usually slaughters, though,

or flays alive.)

Meanwhile, on another end of the glitch:

Something's not right in toxic city.

The water, it clears

into a viral sabotage. . .

IN Steps ECOMAN, *Huge Savings*,

with his purifier scheme

(*glimpses of coinage*).

He mans the canal to this ward

(toxic city).

The victims, bleary-eyed, cheer

and claw for outcomes.

"Excellent".

"They don't taste like rocks."

(*All mutants cheer.*)

TRAPS TO ROUT PHONIES

CARMEN: (*landing in Lady Murasaki's body*). Nurse!

NURSE: Yes, Madam.

(*Temptation is her sideline.*)

CARMEN: What's next on the agenda, Nurse?

(*Woozy, aside, pictures the friends*

she left hanging.) HELP!

(*She knocks Nurse out.*)

Will Carmen be useful in this guise

of ancient wealth

though remote-controlled

a living decoy, all fake?

(*Bubbles up electronically*):

THE INVISIBLE: Materialize. Unfold.

(*Appears: a decoy Carmen, double-jointed and virtual.*

Flips; vanishes.)

Too late. But the clouds
hang slightly on her image still.

SOBA: (*voice off*). That the skin could melt

into pretty jellies, to spread

deliciousness.

CARMEN (as LADY M.): Hey! Quit clipping my tresses!

NURSE: Doctor's orders.

CARMEN: Oh, yeah?

Out in the TIME Capsule:

Mysterious girl, her face zipped in red leather,

pedals through the carnage and flames, she's driven, sneaks

past lab security and — click — starts loading

shopping bags with mutant samples

but not soon enough —

NURSE: Off with the bonnet! (*Aiming.*)

LADY M.: (— *astounded* —). Soba!

(*They kiss, at length. Passionate. Lovemaking flashbacks.*)

SOBA: I was afraid I'd never see you again!

LADY MURASAKI: I didn't know you cared. (*Aside*: Hmmmm.) What

about . . . what's her name . . . Carmen?

SOBA: Who?

LADY M.: Never mind (*grabbing the bags*). You won't get away

with this! Nurses!

But they've gone down with the ship. Lady M. (Carmen) and Soba

huddle close

as the time-swirl breaks open in mid-air: hungering, lathered.

With the bag of tricks, they're vacuumed under (but blissful).

END of Episode.

The ESCAPE of a nurse-liturgical chorus to BANDAGED PARADISE

DOC — CAUGHT (Epilogue)

between savagery and good

(his motto: 'in and out; operate miracles')

his surfaces radiate

hair matches, not for nothing

was he known as — whatever —

plus all the cute mutants he's restored and adopts:

Vermilion-stamped, now shot

at the hands of his own girls

(young, in love, candy-striped)

who — viral— creep

flushing life slowly out.

NURSE CHORUS: Masters, come! Breed us again!

(*Moaning.*)   Keep us rustic, golden messes

                stalked for fun, given plenty of nothing

                fed among dogs and, beauty-

                injected, taught to envy poisons.

SO Young, so mistaken, and so Gauze-Tangled . . .

Identical nurse triplets

(*dewy from sweetness*)

discover and unmuzzle the slave

(gone limp with silence)

(*evocative, dangerous*)

and suddenly, they're run-aways

off to find thrills in the woods!

(*SLAVE lumbers after them.*)

NURSES: (*disguised as unlicensed shepherds —*

in filthy air —

sing). From comfort seethes anguish!

 Curb surgeons by smacks

(with cleavage interspersed).

 To bathe in lavish blisters

 Darken our Instruments.

From foolish adoration to adultering fools . . .

NURSES: (*still singing*). Kiss ambitious invalids,

          collect their spare parts

          while tending new lambs

          and gouging the backsides of wolves.

          Yip-eee!

Slave (as beast) (an ex-libertine) drools lusty; attends,

embossed with mutant gashes, but

ever compact and tuneful

skips alongside, fans them,

declares: What a life!

With his gravy-dunked brain

laughs —

In an economy of glances employed,

hands out medicines; keeps his image up-to-date.

. . . As they gambol on through the butchery pastures . . .

WOODSMAN, full of thirst

but fresh out of manners

and thorny-veined; he'd devour

the nurses, but's held back

by a sudden ringing in his ears.

Becomes love-crippled;

carves songs in the trees.

Song (*infectious*):

A life of spare parts

bucolic-mechanical

happy, happy, and most HAPPY

with flawless complexions

a salary of bruises

though uniformed, quirky, melts:

Uncork and Stomach Us!

(*Hands on hips, all pirouette.*)

KLINK: (*as Slave*).

Pebbles worse than squirrels' teeth,

I eats them — but why?

Luscious, brown — try it.

Quick! I'm late, though maudlin.

(Oh me oh me.)

If I were normaler, I'd linger a while.

NEXT: IDEAL LANDSCAPES (Ecoman's Doing)

OR, *Abstracts harm and leave PITTANCES*:

Benign, benign.

Exposed and ornamented their best sides (bottoms)

all feeling the same, touched, very

unattractive and rural; equipped with casts

who studied realignment, child-cult style

(not by play alone):

NURSE TEAM: Beat us and Join us

        with love, pure, but intentions

        very tainted, a warning: deliver:

        Gullible Trainees: boisterous, ripe,

        (a nice meal for bobcats)

        set up camp against all odds (aforementioned)

        strew flowers, imbibe,

        and counterfeit new memberships.

Nurse-Sorceresses

Swept off, in a fatal craze

(*under orchards, deeper*)

dabbled in blood: who's worse: Mom or child?

Insatiate, herbal and cruel - begin.

The remedy SECRET:

(NURSE 1:) "Sleep a while, next to me."

(NURSE 2:) "If I can keep clean, I'm safe."

Pre-finale: How Anyone ever ended up THERE (In outer-space??)

Sung, in   The more I look, the more I like
unison,
but OFF: the fissures, their shapes,

              dimensionful intentions.

              "Then or whenever

              come and get it."

Led to a Loose Vastness . . .

              Astray - please, please!

              (*Slave kindles the cigarette to C's nipple. She swoons.*)

                 Still Off: Not *ash*tray! (*Doubts sent to abuse true lovers.*)

              Blind/blindfolded —erred—

              bound Nurse Beth, then dipped her low

              (pure-bottomed with shackles)

              (in far and up wet)

(*still sung*): (deeper - Yes.) When lust is high

              all pits are equal.

You-know-who's back, but in a deep freeze:

SHEILA: Catch me if you dare!

Johnny slashes her with his blade a second time.

Lust — tinctured in a jar — drips

to a slight gravity point

tangential and short-sighted

its attribute: distraction.

A profile clock, in random obedience

— that glutinous embrace —

— Ugly, when she thinks —

Out buying up eternities.

The Swamp — where a frog tweaks

her *own*, and KLINK's complexion gets worse

until he falls dumbly in love with that look

fed on recalcitrance

the landscape named "Poisonous"

preventative, gurgles, horizon

AND SO, a complete anesthetic inscribed.

Was it reciprocal?

In cleansed blandness, maybe.

SLAVE: (*Disassembles, then woofs down some (numerous) shavings.*

Knocked out, in formaldehyde.)

      PAY DAY!

KLINK, revealed in a GLISTENING SHEATH

not a drop of shame — resplendent, throned

in a liberty parable

or in electric anguish

Sings: Slip and fall, hobble, PLEAD. (*Repeat.*)

Now IDLE HOPES *in the* ABSENTED *Woods*:

Her dainty bottoms scroll

(*a rose*) (*perfume scatters*)

Swelling, Delicate

in kissing contested:

Left her head right in his fist

(*no brains drip, no blood*),

and the body's just plum gone!

CLASSIC LUSTER

Get it right now:

Her head slips off. He's stumped,

amazed holding the neck.

OTHER ROOF BOOKS

Andrews, Bruce. **Getting Ready To Have Been Frightened**. 116p. $7.50.

Andrews, Bruce. **R & B**. 32p. $2.50.

Bee, Susan [Laufer]. **The Occurrence of Tune**, text by Charles Bernstein. 9 plates, 24p. $6.

Benson, Steve. **Blue Book**. Copub. with The Figures. 250p. $12.50

Bernstein, Charles. **Controlling Interests**. 88p. $6.

Bernstein, Charles. **Islets/Irritations**. 112p. $9.95.

Bernstein, Charles (editor). **The Politics of Poetic Form**. 246p. $12.95; cloth $21.95.

Brossard, Nicole. **Picture Theory**. 188p. $11.95.

Child, Abigail. **From Solids**. 30p. $3.

Davies, Alan. **Active 24 Hours**. 100p. $5.

Davies, Alan. **Signage**. 184p. $11.

Davies, Alan. **Rave**. 64p. $7.95.

Day, Jean. **A Young Recruit**. 58p. $6.

Doris, Stacy. **Kildare**. 104p. $9.95

Dickenson, George-Thérèse. **Transducing**. 175p. $7.50.

DiPalma, Ray. **Raik**. 100p. $9.95.

Dreyer, Lynne. **The White Museum**. 80p. $6.

Edwards, Ken. **Good Science.** 80p. $9.95.

Eigner, Larry. **Areas Lights Heights**. 182p. $12, $22 (cloth).

Estrin, Jerry. **Rome, A Mobile Home.** Copub. with The Figures, O Books, Potes & Poets. 88p. $9.95.

Gizzi, Michael. **Continental Harmonies**. 92p. $8.95.

Gottlieb, Michael. **Ninety-Six Tears**. 88p. $5.

Grenier, Robert. **A Day at the Beach**. 80p. $6.

Hills, Henry. **Making Money**. 72p. $7.50. VHS videotape $24.95. Book & tape $29.95.

Hunt, Erica. **Local History**. 80 p. $9.95.

Inman, P. **Red Shift**. 64p. $6.

Inman, P. **Criss Cross**. 64p. $7.95

Lazer, Hank. **Doublespace**. 192 p. $12.

Legend. Collaboration by Andrews, Bernstein, DiPalma, McCaffery, and Silliman.
  Copub. with L=A=N=G=U=A=G=E. 250p. $12.

Mac Low, Jackson. **Representative Works: 1938–1985**. 360p. $12.95, $18.95 (cloth).

Mac Low, Jackson. **Twenties**. 112p. $8.95.

McCaffery, Steve. **North of Intention**. 240p. $12.95.

Moriarty, Laura. **Rondeaux**. 107p. $8.

Neilson, Melanie. **Civil Noir**. 96p. $8.95.

Pearson, Ted. **Planetary Gear**. 72p. $8.95.

Perelman, Bob. **Face Value**. 72p. $6.

Perelman, Bob. **Virtual Reality**. 80p. $9.95.

Piombino, Nick, **The Boundary of Blur**. 128p. $13.95

Robinson, Kit. **Balance Sheet.** 112 p. $9.95.

Robinson, Kit. **Ice Cubes**. 96p. $6.

Scalapino, Leslie. **Objects in the Terrifying Tense Longing from Taking Place**. 88p. $9.95.

Seaton, Peter. **The Son Master**. 64p. $4.

Sherry, James. **Popular Fiction**. 84p. $6.

Silliman, Ron. **The New Sentence**. 200p. $10.

Silliman, Ron. **N/O**. 112p. $10.95

Templeton, Fiona. **YOU—The City**. 150p. $11.95.

Ward, Diane. **Relation**. 64p. $7.50.

Watten, Barrett. **Progress**. 122p. $7.50.

Weiner, Hannah. **Little Books/Indians**. 92p. $4.

For ordering write:

SEGUE FOUNDATION, ROOF BOOKS, 303 East 8th Street, New York, NY 10009